PRINCETON THEOLOGICAL MONOGRAPH SERIES

Dikran Y. Hadidian

General Editor

21

SEASONS OF THE HEART
In Quest of Faith

SARA HENDERSON HAY
AND NADJA, HER SIAMESE CAT - 1954
Photograph by
Ben Spiegel, 1954

SEASONS OF THE HEART

IN QUEST OF FAITH

Poems by SARA HENDERSON HAY selected and
arranged with biographical memoir by
AGNES DODDS KINARD

PICKWICK PUBLICATIONS
Allison Park, Pennsylvania
1989

Poems by SARA HENDERSON HAY have appeared in the following periodicals: *Voices, Commonweal, The New York American, The New York Times, The New York Herald Tribune, The Christian Century, Harper's Bazaar, Scribner's Magazine, Forum, Good Housekeeping, Canadian Bookman, Kaleidograph Magazine, Bozart, The Miraculous Medal, Poetry World, The Christian Science Monitor, Ladies' Home Journal, Literary Digest, Atlantic Monthly, Psychology, The Saturday Review of Literature, American Poetry Journal, The American Girl, Hygeia, The New York Sun, North American Review, Columbia, Show, The Lyric, Scholastic, The Classmate, Yankee.*
McCall's (1933-1966 - Dedication, Syndicated Column, and Story Hour), *Harper's*, (1931, Sic Transit) and *The New Yorker*, (The Survivor, 1950, by permission © 1950, 1978 Sara Henderson Hay). Additional poems, Special Collection, Carnegie Mellon University Library, Pittsburgh, PA.

Copyright © 1989 by Agnes Dodds Kinard

Published by Pickwick Publications
4137 Timberlane Drive
Allison Park, PA 15101-2932

Library of Congress Cataloging-in-Publication Data

Hay, Sara Henderson
  Seasons of the heart.

  (Princeton theological monograph series ; 21)
  1. Christian poetry, American. I. Kinard, Agnes Dodds.
II. Title. III. Series.
PS3515.A9323S43 1989 811'.52   89-16088
ISBN 1-55635-002-3

To a Southern Lady

who was

SARA HENDERSON HAY

and

To a Southern Gentleman

who is

JAMES PINCKNEY KINARD

CONTENTS

I Desire to Reason With God

Sweet Story of Old

FOREWORD

Perhaps these poems, penned years ago by Sara Henderson Hay, voicing her own dilemmas with her Biblical beliefs, will help others to debate and distill their own convictions of conscience. Today there are sharp ideological conflicts over moral questions such as abortion, capital punishment, nuclear armaments, prayer in the public schools and so on, indicating a deep concern among the citizens on problems of ethics, if not of religion itself.

This memoir accompanies a selection of her poems about people and events in the Bible, with related verses about Faith, some inspirational some disputational, but relevant to one's reading of the Old and New Testaments.

The literary quality of the verses is uneven as the poems were written at different stages of the development of Sara Henderson Hay from a talented precocious seven-year-old poet into the accomplished artist she became. Her patterns remained constant, she did not care to attempt "free verse", but her insights varied from caring about simple tangible natural things to challenging accepted reactions to dogma and tradition. Irony and satire in her work became more pronounced over the years, while her sly wit and gentle nature were continuously revealed in her six volumes of poetry.

All of her books: *Field of Honor, This My Letter, The Delicate Balance, The Stone and the Shell, Story Hour* and *A Footing on this Earth,* all are out of print. Alas. . .

Pittsburgh is the city of her birth and early childhood but Anniston, Alabama, home of her mother and grandmother, was the home of her heart making her the cultured, charming Southern lady she remained until her death. Someone said "She likes carefully wrought simplicity, the classic, and the ceremonious. She also likes courtesies."

We were friends of many years, good but not intimate friends. While she and I were native Pittsburghers, Sally and James Kinard, my husband, shared a Southern background. Friends though we were, it was not until after her death July 7, 1987, at age 80, that I learned she had never had the "small son" of whom she wrote so eloquently, so maternally, in poem after poem, some twenty in all. They are so poignant I could not bring myself to mention her child to her as she never mentioned him to me, although we did talk of other sad personal experiences in her life before she came back to Pittsburgh as the bride of Nikolai Lopatnikoff.

In the South it is customary to use two first names, so it was "Sara Henderson," never just "Sara," signed to gifts of collections of her poems encased in tooled leather volumes, one presented to "Dear Daddy" on Father's Day, and fourteen "To my most beloved mother" . . . . The Southern drawl in her voice became more pronounced when she and my husband reminisced about Charleston, South Carolina, and other places, and so it was that to us Sara Henderson Hay Lopatnikoff was "Sa 'Hensn" while to other friends in Pittsburgh she was Sally Lopatnikoff.

Sara Henderson Hay Lopatnikoff was history-oriented, saving each scrap of memorabilia or evidence of her long literary career as poet and critic. I was with her the day in August, 1987, after she turned over to Carnegie Mellon University her notebooks, scrap books and papers (in advance of her bequest). She said to me "I have just given away my life". Now, through the voluminous papers of Sara Henderson Hay in the Rare Book Room of the Hunt Library, Carnegie Mellon University, I read her business letters, articles, manuscripts, news clippings and other memorabilia, gaining new insight into her business acumen, and into her character and personality, beyond the warm acquaintance with the verses in her volumes fondly inscribed to my husband and me.

I am impressed now by her modesty which made no reference to her unique, historic, experiences when at the age of 28, she was privileged to meet with many of the political leaders of Europe, as I learned only from her diary of that pre-World War II period. My idea has been to let Sally speak for herself, from her diary, letters, her writings, news clippings, interviews and handwritten copy books--all so meticulously documented, saved and arranged by her and given to Carnegie Mellon University–perhaps for this very purpose. And so I say "thank you, Sally . . . " and thank you Carnegie Mellon University, specifically Mary Catherine Johnsen, Librarian of the Rare Books at the Hunt Library, and Thomas J. Mickalak, Director of Libraries.

Appreciation is due also to Frederick Hetzell, Director of the University of Pittsburgh Press and to Paul Roberts, Editor of the magazine of the Historical Society of Western Pennsylvania for their valuable guidance. Composer Roland Leich of Carnegie Mellon University added interesting musical notes. My special thanks to Willa Hay Godfrey, the poet's sister, for her generous approval and gracious sharing of recollections and personal poems such as *Little Prayer* and *'Til Death Us Do Part*.

Though now residing elsewhere, Pittsburgh Bibliophile Tom Ross gave his talent and his time in creating the design of *Seasons of the Heart* in honor of former member Sara Henderson Hay. Thos. C. Pears III, has added helpful suggestions.

Although we too are members of the Bibliophiles it was the Reverend Jon Clifton's introduction to Dikran Y. Hadidian which led to the happy collaboration in this publication by Pickwick Publications, to which I say Hallelujah!

Agnes Dodds Kinard

SARA HENDERSON HAY
1906 - 1987

The Poet and The Person

Biographical Memoir by Agnes Dodds Kinard

Sara Henderson Hay, author of six volumes of award-winning poetry, is often called a Pittsburgh poet, but her work speaks to the concerns of people everywhere. She herself often insisted that she was a poet who just happened to live in Pittsburgh.

Hailed in 1966 by long-time Pittsburgh history writer Robert Alberts as "one of the nation's foremost poets," she was the great-granddaughter of Alexander Hay, mayor of the city from 1842 to 1844. She was born November 13, 1906, in Pittsburgh to Major Watson Hay and Daisy Baker Hay of Anniston, Alabama. Sara Henderson spent her early childhood years in smoky, industrial Pittsburgh, and made numerous visits with her mother to relatives in Anniston. The visits became more and more frequent and finally Sara Henderson, her sister Willa, and their mother remained in Anniston and lived with Daisy Baker Hay's mother. The father corresponded faithfully, sending regular

1

checks, and there was no divorce. Spending her formative adolescence in the South, with its leisurely pace, was a permanent influence on the poet. Throughout her life, even in business letters, she was gracious and charming in the southern manner. In keeping with southern custom, she was called "Sara Henderson," instead of "Sara."

A collection of her business papers, a diary and scrapbooks with press clippings covering the highlights of her career was willed to Hunt Library at Carnegie Mellon University, and the excerpts for this essay were drawn from that material. Three years before her death in 1987 at age 80, Sara Henderson Hay wrote a letter that was read at ceremonies marking the 85th anniversary of the Wilkinsburg Library in suburban Pittsburgh.

> "Since my early childhood, the written word, in books, has always had for me an utter magic," the poet recalled. "Long before I could read, my mother read to me, mostly poetry, the sonorous rhythms of Evangeline, the lovely and now out of fashion lines of Tennyson and Swinburne, even Shakespeare . . . . Poetry was my first love . . .
> "And when I could read myself . . . the Carnegie Library (in Anniston) was where I spent a charmed time, heading to it when school was out, and on Saturday mornings standing bemused, trying to choose which of all the wealth of high adventure, fantasy, romance and exotic far away places and lives I could take home with me . . . . I don't know whether children today find a book the marvelous thing it was before ra-

dio, television and movies were available.
I hope they do."

By age 10, Sara Henderson was a "published poet," receiving $20 for a poem about golf published in *Judge Magazine*. In June 1921 she earned a grade school diploma from the Thomas Wightman School in Pittsburgh. She attended high school in Anniston, and her mother continued to send her poems to the *Anniston Star*, which had come to consider her its own protegee.

At Brenau College in Georgia, Sara Henderson Hay was editor of the college magazine, an unusual distinction for a freshman. After transferring to Columbia University, her writing skills were honed under the tutelage of Professors John Erskine, Joseph Auslander and Hoxie Fairchild. Her poems appeared in the college magazine and the publication of the *Parnassus Club*, a club for young women where she lived and waited tables to help pay her room and board of $16 per week. She received her bachelor's degree in 1929.

In 1931 alone four anthologies included her poetry: *Selected Magazine Verse* for 1931, *Younger Poets, Anthology of Garden Verse* and *Columbia University Poets*. Through Harold Vinal, editor of *Voices: A Journal of Poetry*, which also had published her work, she was introduced to New York literary circles and joined The Poetry Society of America.

Her first selection of 66 poems was chosen in a contest from among 207 entries and was published as a book in 1933 by Kaleidograph Press. *The*

3

Field of Honor was dedicated to "One Who Never Laughed at me, and To One Who Did"—her mother and Hoxie Fairchild, respectively. The title for the critically acclaimed collection was chosen from the title of a tripartite poem about love foresworn for honor.

FIELD OF HONOR

I

In truth, we might have seen it, from the start.
This path would have its turning; there would be
No real alternative for you and me
Fashioned of honest earth, except to part.
Whether the blow were mine to deal, or whether
Yours the swift blade by which this bond were
      sundered,
The hearts must bleed, because the feet have
      blundered
Into a way we may not walk together

Rebuke me not, beloved, in that I
Perforce do quickly that which needs must be;
I am as one who fights because she fears
A darker wound, a deadlier agony
Than fronts her now—and if I say good-by,
Believe me that I say it through my tears.

II

I do beseech that you belive me true,
And cry solace in my desperate need.
My dearest love, I had been false indeed
If I did *not* this bitter thing I do.
Better a thousand times the anguish due,
The heart insolvent, but the spirit freed,
Than turn this traitor to a certain creed,
And faithless to myself, as well as you.

For it were surely treachery most base
To risk the sullying of so proud a shield;
To chance a single stain upon my face
Of what we bear in honor from the field,
Worthy to keep untarnished through the years.
Though polished daily with what meed of tears.

III

Strange paradox, my friend, that you and I
Who deemed our trusted strength so sure and sweet,
Must find ourselves stricken to earth thereby,
Our swords turned sharply to our own defeat.
"Wisdom" writ large across the frozen breast
Is doubtful comfort when the heart is breaking;
What final irony is manifest
That we are scourged with thongs of our own making.

So I shall nevermore behold your face,
Nor look for heaven at your fingertips;
And all my ordered goings shall attest
How I have set mine honor in its place!
Albeit by the blood upon my lips,
Albeit by the ashes in my breast.

One poem, reflecting her life-long love of animals, most requested for republication is:

For a Dead Kitten

Put the rubber mouse away,
Pick the spools up from the floor,
What was velvet-shod, and gay,
Will not want them, any more--

What was warm, is strangely cold.
Whence was dissolved the little breath?
How could this small body hold
So immense a thing as Death?

After graduation from Columbia, Sara Henderson Hay worked at Charles Scribner's & Sons, first as a secretary in the editorial offices, then in the bookstore and later in the Rare Book Department, while doing free-lance proofreading and editing. She carefully aimed her poems so rejections were few: biblical poems appeared in the *Churchman* and similar publications, while the New Yorker published witty, worldly verses.

One editorial job she enjoyed most was editing and proofreading a gigantic volume, Burton E. Stevenson's *Home Book of Shakespeare Quotations*. Being "a pushover for a quotation," the poet recognized them "as among the richest lodes in all the mines of literature" and collected her own treasury of "things supremely well said, witty, wise, kindly or malicious, that can be lifted out of context and admired for themselves or applied wherever suitable."

Much of her poetry shows this fascination with Shakespeare and other classicists, superimposed on a firm foundation of stories, parables and verses from the King James Bible, which her mother read as lullabies to her as a child. In notes for one of her readings, the poet wrote that the "marvelous imagery of the King James Old and New Testaments . . . made a deep impression on me . . . . Of course the Holy Family, from the angle of their human-ness, offer endless material for thought ".

In her volumes the poet expressed her love of nature, her concern for the underdog, her love of love and her distrust of it. Her verses display a vibrant warmth, and we are fortunate that her ideas about creating poetry have been preserved in her collection at Hunt Library. As early as the mid-1950s, she observed that "what is apt to come under fire today is not the technical pattern of a poem, but any tendency of its author to be warmly and directly and candidly emotional.

"Ingenuous and uncomplicated sentiment is, in these days, very likely to be miscalled sentimentality." The two, insisted the poet, are "something very different indeed."

Several newspapers besides the *Anniston Star* followed Sara Henderson Hay's early career, including the *Atlanta Journal* and the *Birmingham New Age Herald*. Both papers commented on her beauty and charm, as well as her poetry, as she traveled the South receiving accolades and promoting her books.

A syndicated columnist for the Birmingham paper, Gladys Baker (no relation), who was a Barbara Walters of the day, gave the 28-year old poet the opportunity to experience the high adventure and exotic travel that she had fantasized about during her childhood reading sessions at the library. Gladys Baker was a renowned interviewer of George Bernard Shaw, Albert Einstein, Eleanor Roosevelt, Babe Ruth and other luminaries of the 1930s, and she engaged the poet as her secretary and companion. On assignment for the *New York Times*, the pair began a trip in 1935 that would take them across much of Europe.

Arriving in Turkey on May 18, they registered at the Park Hotel, Istanbul's newest. "Having late dinner, President Mustafa Kemal (Ataturk) came in!" Sara Henderson Hay noted in her diary. "With all his entourage, generals, Deputies, etc. . . . Invited us over to his table (luckily we had evening clothes on), seated us one at his right, one on his left . . . ." "Ataturk, she wrote, "knew who Gladys was, and she made the most terrific impression! He talked with her, through his secretary, until seven in the morning. In the meantime, we'd danced, and breakfast was served as the sunlight came over the Bosphorus. Remarkable man, drank raki all night and we'd never have known it. (Bed at 9:30 a.m.)"

The interview appeared under the Times headline: "War Peril Great, Ataturk Declares;" Ataturk said that "in the event of war in the area the United States could not remain aloof or neutral."

The Turkish dictator's influence extended to Rumania, where they also were received as official guests. Interviewed there were the former international playboy King Carol, Queen Marie and others in the royal family. In Austria, Chancellor Kurt von Schuschnigg declared that the Nazi movement in his country was kept alive by outside propaganists and financial support from across the German border.

Scheduled interviews with top Nazi leaders–Hitler, Goering and Goebbles–fell through because the three were out of Berlin. Hay wrote in her diary that she wished she knew the city's undercurrents. "On the surface all is quiet and very peaceful. It's hard to realize that this Germany is the country that everyone in the world is watching with distrust and fear. We don't even see many soldiers on the street.

"When we came into Germany we were awfully nervous about our notes–remembering all the newspaper stories of people thrown into jail for criticizing the Nazis. The night before we got into Berlin we went through (our) papers, put the negative ones in an envelope in the bottom of the office"–probably a suitcase separate from their trunks and other bags–"and I wore the others inside my vest!. . . . We got the papers in without any trouble."

In Rome, interviews with Pope Pius XI and Mussolini were granted. Asked on June 23, 1935, about the potential for Italy waging war in Abyssinia, Mussolini bridled and replied: "I said Italy will never perpetrate war, but her colonies must be defended." Soon afterwards Italian planes were strafing Ethiopian warriors in their African tribal battle finery.

9

Mixed with the talk of war in the diary are mentions of social events, such as the opera "Aida" in Vienna and a Beethoven concert in London: "All this music is good for me, and what's more, I like it." Before boarding the SS Normandie for the United States, the correspondents visited London's Cheshire Cheese, a pub dating to 1669 and haunt of Johnson, Goldsmith and later literary notables.

Sara Henderson Hay returned to Scribner's, writing poetry and reviewing poetry and fiction for the *Saturday Review of Literature* and other magazines. Her second book, *This My Letter*, was published by Alfred A. Knopf, in 1939, with the title from lines by John Donne. The book was dedicated to Raymond Holden. As a *Saturday Review* editor, he had turned down what she considered some of her most profound poems, preferring to print those about her "small son." She went to a lecture at which Raymond Holden was the speaker. In an interview with the *Anniston Star*, the poet recalled that he had asked, "How is your small son, Mrs. Hay?" "It isn't Mrs Hay. I'm not married, you see." Then laughing at the editor's eyebrows, she added, "and I haven't any son. Mr. Holden, you, a poet, should know that having brain children now and then is our license."

The exact date of the first meeting with Holden, a 1915 Princeton graduate, poet, and author of an Abraham Lincoln biography, was not recorded. But on May 9, 1937, they were married by a justice of peace in Geenwich, Connecticut. It was his third marriage.

Other readers also believed in the son's existence, so moving were her verses. Toys, cookies and similar gifts were sent to the poet "mother." Fifteen poems in *This My Letter* involved the imaginary child, such as "Following the Small Son to Church" and:

To My Small Son, Growing Up
'But when I become a man, I put away childish things. . .'

1 Corinthians 13:11

God grant he may not lose them yet,
All of the little childish things.
I cannot bear that he forget
His young and brave imaginings.

That, growing up, he loses them quite:
The splendid marching days that pass,
The Pirate in the wind at night,
The curious, friendly-fingered grass.

Is it such wisdom, that he can
At so great price become a man?

The book received laudatory reviews. In the *New York Herald Tribune Books* of October 9, 1939, Ruth Lechlitner commented that "as in her first book . . . Miss Hay's best poems are those based on religious subjects or biblical references. The lyrics in the concluding pages of *This My Letter* have a beautiful simplicity, candor, homely tenderness, with an ironic insight that turns their edges sharply from the sentimental."

In letters and lectures, the poet explained her interest in biblical subjects: "I found myself troubled by the predicaments that many of the characters found themselves in . . . and I couldn't help but be somewhat taken aback by the quite implacable punishment occasionally dealt out by Jehovah." She wondered about Abraham's near-sacrifice of his son Isaac: "What was the effect of the experience on the little boy . . . ?"

She was curious about overlooked biblical characters, as well: "the innocent bystanders, so to speak, who witnessed the miracles, who saw Jesus pass by and who went on their way. I've often wondered what became of them, whether they remembered anything about the experience, or Him . . . ." She wished "to speak a word in the defence of some of those whom I felt had been rather put upon, the underdogs, the misunderstood or unfairly treated, those made an example of . . . ."

Although critics singled out the volume's biblical poems for praise, it contained poems that helped to establish other themes that Sara Henderson Hay would return to throughout her career:

The Song
(for R.H.)

Loving you is like hearing a sound breaking
In a great wave of music on the ears:
The exquisite movement of music that brings tears
To the eyes, too beautiful to be borne, waking
Such rapture in the breast as wrings the heart.
Oh sweet, oh most beloved, this loving you
Is music, but more than music--having no part
With ceasing, with dying away as melodies do,

Having some quality more pure and strong,
More passionate and durable and true

To sound across my days my whole life long
Its breathing cadence, its enduring song.

But the song did not endure. The marriage ended in divorce in 1949, the year the following poem was written:

Residence: Washoe County, Nevada. . .

Weep no more, my lady, this gaudy city
Blossoms for you beneath those out-size stars;
Here no one cares, and there's no room for pity
Around the gambling tables and at the bars.
The lightening fingered men with the open collars
Can deal more quickly than your eyes can move
And here they give your change in silver dollars,
Heavy as hearts are, and more lasting than love.

The lawyer finishes, even while you speak,
Making his notes. He's heard it all before.
All that to you was terrible and unique
Is an old story, lady; weep no more,
In six weeks you can lay your burden down.
Down by the Riverside Hotel, in town.

In notes from one of her readings, she said many poems add "to the lineaments of the Self Portrait which all books of poetry really are. Not all poems are autobiographical or even from the poet's personal experience," she said, but the importance of such poems could be seen "to the discerning eye which reads between the lines."

With the world's attention riveted on the global struggle of the early 1940s, Sara Henderson Hay's poetry voiced many Americans' preoccupation with the war. "Black Out," minus the first verse, appeared in the *New Yorker*. "Blood Donor" and "To the Nazi Leaders" were printed in the *New York Herald Tribune*. They all evoke the feelings and fears of the era.

To the Nazi Leaders
"The evil that men do. . ."

The evil these men did in their dark time
Lives after them in their infected state.
They were the leaders, but the people's crime
Is that they followed and they called them great.

These are the men whose monstrous alchemy
Gave what is worst in all a shape and name--
What ailed the people, but the people's crime
Corruption's color and the face of shame?

These were the leaders--they were fortunate
Because they shall not live more lives than one
To look upon the work their hands have done.
These are the people who must expiate
The guilt they shared when they did not distain
The bloody hand and fellowship of Cain.

One poem, "The Neighbors," published in *Good Housekeeping* in 1943, was attacked by some religious organizations for surmising what might have been the reaction of neighbors of Mary and Joseph to their Son's degrading crucifixion between thieves. In the controversial passage an imaginary neighbor says of Jesus, "He'd a' been a better son if he'd stayed home and raised a family like his brothers done." *The Acolyte*, the official organ of the National Organization for Decent Literature sponsored by Bishop John F. Noll, called the use of "brothers" blasphemous.

Evidently the *The Acolyte's* editors took their objection up with the editors of *Good Housekeeping*, who apologized to Bishop Noll. The inside story on the brouhaha was detailed by Drew Pearson, in his syndicated column, "Merry Go Round" of March 25, 1943. But according to George Seldes' magazine, In Fact, newspapers in many parts of the country suppressed the column. Clippings in Sara Henderson Hay's scrapbook related the episode.

These years were full of crises and conflicts for the poet. Her third book, published in 1951 by Scribner's, contained only 42 poems. Dedicated to her mother, *The Delicate Balance* received the Edna St. Vincent Millay Memorial Award from The Poetry Society of America. The title was contained in the last verse of the poem, "Bottle Should Be Plainly Labeled Poison":

> There is a delicate balance set
> Between Hope's virtue and its vice
> The man who takes it to forget
> Must know how little will suffice.

The strengths of *The Delicate Balance* were evident. *New York Times* critic Robert Hayden wrote: "One is impressed by the poet's moral earnestness, insight and by her feeling of irony and paradox . . . One of Miss Hay's assets is her skillfulness in fusing the serious and the humorous in the same poem." Another eminent critic, Louis Untermeyer, said about the book: "It not only lives up to but completely illustrates its title. Delicacy is the keynote of these poems, but it is a delicacy balanced between frail whimsicality and fine-spun strength . . ."

The poet, in her business papers, outlined the strict standards and disciplined thought that underlay the delicacy of her verse: "A poem should be able to recreate in the mind of its reader as nearly as possible what the poet felt when he wrote it." She sought "a line or two or three lines embodying the central idea of the point of the poem." The point, she added, "need not be stated directly; it may be presented subtly or obliquely or by suggestion or by allusion or metaphor, but what it says should never, in essence, be confused or incompletely realized by its author, or be undisciplined and full of loose inconsistencies which sound impressive but cannot bear analysis."

Receiving a fellowship to pursue her writing, Sara Henderson Hay spent the summer of 1950 at the MacDowell Colony in Peterborough, New Hampshire, where she met widower Nikolai Lopatnikoff, also a resident there. The Russian-American composer of classical music, twice a Guggenheim fellow, was a professor of composition in the Department of Music at the Carnegie Institute of Technology in Pittsburgh.

Born in Estonia in 1903, Lopatnikoff had

lived in Finland, Germany and France before arriving in the United States in 1939, becoming an American citizen on D-Day, 1944. Educated as a civil engineer like his father, Lopatnikoff composed his first symphony while studying in Germany. A sonata for violin and strings, written in 1948, was published in 1951 with a dedication to Sara Henderson Hay. The couple married in New York in January of that year, and then returned to the bride's city of birth, making their home at 5448 Bartlett Street on the edge of Schenley Park. Their garden attracted rabbits and squirrels, while in the house there was always at least one resident cat.

Although her husband did not write music to accompany her poems, a number of others did. One of the first was Kenneth Walton, who in 1939 wrote music for "Mary–Sacred Song." Among her other biblical poems set to music were "The Ten Lepers," Bethlehem," "While Joseph Slept," "The Silent Ones," "The Gifts," and "The Child."

The Carnegie Mellon association resulted in 34 of her poems being teamed with a varied group of musical scores by CMU Professor Roland Leich. Sometimes serious, sometimes playful, some were orchestral and some were for male chorus or Pittsburgh's Mendelssohn Choir. One of the most appealing was the 1956 transposition of the poem "For a Dead Kitten" into a lullaby. The collaboration also resulted in a work for voice and strings, with support in 1979 from the Pennsylvania Council on the Arts. A composer the couple encountered at the MacDowell Colony was Paul Amadeus Pisk, a former student of Arnold Schoenberg in Austria. Around 1958 Pisk composed music for nine poems by Sara Henderson Hay.

There were interesting collaborations throughout her career. At the invitation of Samuel Hazo, director of the International Poetry Forum, she contributed verses for a musical composition, "The Pickle Suite." It was premiered by Robert Boudreau's American Wind Symphony Orchestra in 1969 as a kind of inside joke saluting the orchestra's major benefactor, H. J. Heinz II, chairman of Pittsburgh's H. J. Heinz Co.

The Pickle

Since man has always been enticed
By what's provocatively spiced,
Some clever cook, his taste to tickle,
Ingeniously devised the PICKLE.

The pickle hot, the pickle chilly,
The cauliflower, the pickallilly
The garlic dill, in jar or firkin,
The crisp and aromatic Gherkin,

The pickled peach, the pickled pear,
The watermelon pickle fair,
And even, in peppercorns and brine,
The pickled trotter of the swine!

Oh savory relish, guaranteed
To waken, with the greatest speed,
A palate dull or fickle,
Accept our praise: for sour, for sweet,
Garnish of salad, boon to meat,

The condiment which, I repeat,
Makes even the humblest snack complete--
Th' Incomparable Pickle!

In her long marriage to a composer, she
wrote more than 40 witty limericks about the colorful lives and foibles of the classical composers. They
appeared in *Musical Journal*, published by Hamp-
ton International Communications, Inc. The mas-
ter copy, bound in yellow flowered cotton cloth, is
among her papers at Hunt Library.

Lives of the Composers

Said Liszt to the Countess, "We two
Make a wonderful couple it's true,
But I hardly need mention
I had no intention
Of breathing that binding "I do!"

To which she responded, "I knew
From the start you might bid me adieu,
But as proof of our trysts
I have three little Liszts,
Which will help to remind me of you."

Nikolai and Sally Lopatnikoff (the poet continued publishing under "Sara Henderson Hay") returned to the MacDowell Colony two summers in
the 1950s, but it was in 1959 at the Huntington Hart-
ford Foundation in Pacific Palisades, California, (a
west coast equivalent to the MacDowell Colony)
that she wrote 18 poems for her next volume. That
year the University of Pittsburgh Press published
The Stone and The Shell, the Press' first book of

poetry. It received the Pegasus Award in 1960 and included two poems which won individual recognition: "Elegy," winner of the John David Leitch Memorial Prize in 1955 and "Witness for the Defence," winner of the Lyric Memorial Prize in 1959.

The book was dedicated to the poet's husband, and in publicity, as well as on the book's cover, she requested that it be noted that "she is the wife of Nikolai Lopatnikoff, the noted Russian-American composer and professor of music at Carnegie Mellon Institute of Technology."

In mid-1959 a three column review of the book appeared in the *Pittsburgh Press*. Yvonne Wallace described the ambience of the Lopatnikoffs' home and noted a ridged rock that the poet had placed in the nature of a touchstone from Steeple-top, the home of Edna St. Vincent Millay. "Like Emily Dickinson who 'could see heaven in a grain of sand,' Sally finds metaphysical meaning in stones, shells, animals, people," Wallace wrote. "Her province is the world of nature and man's relation to that world, to his gods and to his fellow creatures."

In her own papers, the poet elaborated: "Rhythm is a part of man's very life; he has always carried on his life in accord with the obvious and regular alternations of day and night, and the fixed sequences of the seasons. Rhythm is in his heart beat and his breath and his pulse. We tend to speak rhythmically; and to see things in patterns and order." She described her preference for a poetic landscape with "figures—human or bird or beast or. . . stones and shells," and she was "inclined to look for some tie-up with human nature. . . because I recognize in myself that age-old instinct of man to identify, to attach himself to the world about him, to stake his claim in Time."

One poem in the fourth book was:

The Enemy

It was not grief I died of, no, nor love,
Not even when he set his heel upon my heart;
Nor any crowding fury that could move
Within my breast to tear my breast apart.
Not thirst, nor starving want, nor bitter need
Accomplished my demise, nor wounds unmended,
So long as these could wring me, then indeed
I was alive; by no such means was ended.

None of these things contrived to bring me low.
Time, whom I trusted, was my deadly foe,
And he it was whose daily anodyne
Numbed the live nerve itself against the living pain
And stilled the rage, and quenched, and fed, and
        healed me
Of all my hurts and, with the healing, killed me.

The poet also wrote prose. The work of another Pittsburgh-born poet, Robinson Jeffers, contained strong nature and metaphysics themes, and Sara Henderson Hay examined his work in an article in *Famous Men and Women of Pittsburgh*, published in 1981. Early in her career she had a short mystery story published in Ellery Queen Magazine but decided the short story was not her province. She also wrote for magazines.

In a *Carnegie Tech Quarterly* article in 1961 she recounted Pittsburgh's role in "what is probably

21

the wittiest and best sustained literary hoax of our times . . . ." The hoax began in 1916 with the appearance of *Spectra: New Poems* by Emanuel Morgan and Anne Knish–far out verse praised by many leading critics. Sketchy biographies in the book claimed the authors were Pittsburghers, but no Pittsburghers had heard of them. The article revealed that the real authors were the brilliant young poets Witter Byner and Arthur Davison Ficke, who "outraged by the charlatanism of some of the new 'schools'. . . . produced a deliberate parody to render such schools patently ridiculous. (. . . in some ten days of hilarious industry, helped by ten quarts of excellent scotch.)"

To handle the flood of correspondence caused by the book's success, the conspirators enlisted the aid of the wife of Edmond Esquerre, then professor of chemistry at Carnegie Tech. Posing as Morgan, she replied for nearly two years to letters, questions about the "Spectrists" and requests for more poems, which Byner supplied.

Edgar Lee Masters called the Spectric theory "'an idea capable of great creative development'. . ." and Harvard Professor Amy Lowell, distrustful at the beginning, eventually recommended the volume to students. The episode, Sara Henderson Hay concluded, "cleared the air of a great deal of poetic pretension and attitudinizing . . ."

She was among those who criticized "obscurist" poetry. "As you may have gathered from my previous reviews, and if you have read any of my own work," she wrote to a budding Idaho poet in 1942, "I am not a follower of the obscurist school of poetry. The poetry which means most to me says something to me directly and clearly; it doesn't leave me groping in a fog of high-sounding abstractions and esoteric allusions." She admitted she was not a good judge of highly impressionistic verse that has come to dominate modern poetry. Instead, she sought "to strike an answering chord" in readers by building her poems around the "universals of human experience: love, grief, the tragedy of war, the mysteries of life and death."

Story Hour was Sara Henderson Hay's fifth volume, published by Doubleday in 1963. It was dedicated to her sister, Willa Hay Godfrey and differed from her earlier works in that only one poem has a biblical reference:

Dedication
I Kings 1:1-3

To all the luckless suitors who died trying
To scale the slope of glass;
To poor Rapunzel, in her tower sighing,
To Abelard, at Mass;
To Dido, on the headlands, hearing the dying
Sound of the oarlock's ring;
And little Abishag, into her pillows crying,
Warming an old, cold King. . . .

The volume has a dominant theme: a critical look at the psychological and moral values inherent in familiar fairy tales such as "Jack and the Beanstalk," "The Three Litte Pigs," "Blue Beard," etc. The book's title was that of a poem which appeared in *McCalls* in 1959:

Story Hour

He swung the axe, the toppling beanstalk fell.
Hurrah, Hurrah for Jack, the self-reliant.
The Townsfolk gathered to wish him well.
Was no one sorry for the murdered giant?
Did no one, as the news spread far and wide,
Protest the means Jack took to gold and glory:
Guile, trespass, robbery and homicide?
It is not mentioned in the popular story.

Dear Child, leave off such querries and suggestions,
And let that gullible innocence prevail
Which, in the Brother Grimms' and our own time,
Applauds the climber, and ignores the crime.
How requisite to every fairy tale
A round-eyed Listener, with no foolish questions.

Syndicated Column

Dear Worried: Your husband's actions aren't unique,
His jealousy's a typical defense.
He feels inadequate, in consequence,
He broods. (My column, by the way, last week
Covered the subject fully.) I suggest
You reassure him; work a little harder
To build his ego, stimulate his ardor.
Lose a few pounds, and try to look your best.
As for his growing a beard, and dyeing it blue,
Merely a bid for attention; nothing wrong with him.
Stop pestering him about that closet, too.
If he wants to keep it locked, why go along with
      him.

24

Just be the girl he married; don't nag, don't pout.
Cheer up. And let me know how things work out.

Many of the poems in *Story Hour* were
sought for re-publication in anthologies, textbooks
and other educational materials for use in high
schools and other classes. "The Builders," a take-off
on "The Three Little Pigs," was one of the most often reprinted. The psychological themes were taken
up by doctors and psychiatrists, used as texts for papers presented at medical conventions, for instance,
by Dr. Richard Day, head of Pediatrics at the University of Pittsburgh Medical Center.

In a letter to the poet, Ogden Nash wrote,
"Your verses were the first that have stimulated me
into emitting a quote in many years . . . . "

Seven of the book's poems were choreo-
graphed into a ballet which opened in Washington,
D.C., and played as late as 1970. Washington Post reviewer Jean Battey applauded the Ethel Butler
Company for its premiere of the "marvelous dance
work," calling it,"one of the most interesting works
I have seen produced on the Washington scene . . .
set to some bitter and bitting parodies of nursery
rhymes and stories . . ."

Story Hour poems also provided inspiration
for the popular NBC television progam "That Was
the Week That Was," featuring Burr Tilstrom with
his hand puppets: "The Only Son," about Tom
Thumb, with its anti-mom message, was the topic
of one program. A live interview by Barbara Walters on "The Today Show" also helped to promote
the book.

The poet said she mined nursery rhymes and fairy tales because they provided "familiar dramatic personae." Her poems were not "for children, and though they are ostensibly light verse, they are really in deadly earnest, because I wanted to point out in these extraordinary situations and curious ethics and moralities a parallel in contemporary human nature . . ."

As Story Hour spread her name, Governor William Scranton in 1963 honored her as a "Distinguished Daughter of Pennsylvania."

Three years later came her last book, *A Footing on This Earth*, published by Doubleday. That year *Pittsburgh Quote* called her one of the nation's foremost poets, and the *Anniston Star*–in her other "hometown"–editorialized: "Miss Hay's delightful sense of humour must have been tickled to find herself listed, along with steel mills, rivers, great buildings, fields and mountains, as a municipal asset, but . . . Pittsburgh is to be commended on its wisdom in surveying its 'natural assets.' We are proud to claim our share of one."

The book was dedicated to her mother and the memory of her father, who had died in 1938. In a letter to her publisher, the poet noted that "Footing came out before Mother was taken ill–She was very happy about it." The *Quote* article probably was sent to the *Anniston Star* by Daisy Baker Hay, the last of 60 years of news items about her poet daughter she had supplied the paper.

The official bulletin of The Poetry Society of America in February 1967 said of *Footing*:

These poems (almost 200 of them) range over a period of 34 years, a good record in survival for a poet. Miss Hay's competence has been evident throughout these years. . . She is a mistress of the quick quatrain, the small pithy image, the traditional lyric posture. She has wit, deftness, and is always ladylike and charming.

Reviewer Edith Lovejoy Pierce said in the *Christian World* that the book was

only one step below the first rung of Jacob's ladder. . . Her light verse is deceptively knotty. . . Her religious poetry asks pointed questions. Always sensitive to human sorrows and problems, she takes the part of Man (or perhaps more accurately Woman) against God, or God as he is often inadequately conceived in a rather simplistic reading of the Bible. But whether or not one quarrels with her theology on occasion, one cannot fault her on the expression of it, which is sometimes startling and often moving. How far is poetic license allowed in biblical interpretation? Very far, this poet must admit! This book speaks mainly to exiles from Eden of whom there are more abroad than most authors and publishers seem willing to acknowledge.

Into the 1960s and 1970s Sara Henderson Hay accepted invitations to speak and read her poems to a wide variety of audiences, including poetry societies, libraries, alumnae groups, church groups, and university associations nationwide. (Audio recordings of some of her readings are at Farleigh Dickinson College and the Library of Congress.) She also wrote book reviews for magazines and was generous with advice to aspiring poets.

> It is a pity, I think, that this fear of being old-
> fashioned or sentimental can persuade a poet to
> abandon a natural simplicity for a contrived
> complexity," she wrote to one young poet. She
> added: "The contemporary saying, 'Do your own
> thing' is good advice, if you are sure it is your
> own thing . . . . I've always felt it unfair for a
> poem to appear, as they sometimes do today, to
> be merely the rough materials of a poem, the
> jotted down notes, the unorganized stuff which
> the poet hasn't taken the time or trouble to sort
> out, but depended on the reader to draw his own
> conclusions as to the meaning. This kind of im-
> provisation is present in a great deal of contem-
> porary art—music, painting, sculpture, as well
> as in poetry.

For artists to be able to communicate well, she added, required "a quality of receptive attention, of alert interest, of active participation."

The Lopatnikoffs were prominent in the cultural life of Pittsburgh; the "society pages" of the newspapers reported what Sally wore at the opening symphony concert of the season and so on. She chaired "The Silhouettes," a musical lecture series about forthcoming programs of the Pittsburgh Symphony Orchestra and Nikolai was featured speaker concerning his compositions to be performed by the Symphony under the direction of Dr. William Steinberg. A member of the National Society of Arts and Letters, the poet was also active with the Pittsburgh Bibliophiles.

In 1969 Nikolai's retirement from teaching freed the couple to travel more frequently in Europe, which they enjoyed until his death in 1976 after 25 years of marriage.

The poet continued accepting invitations to speak until 1978, when she wrote disappointed administrators at Bellarmine College in Louisville, Kentucky, that "believing with Emily Dickinson that 'capacity to terminate is a specific grace . . . ' I choose to bow out while both I myself and my audience enjoy the performance."

Recognition continued. In 1980 *The Kentucky Poetry Review* published a special "sara henderson hay" issue, with an introduction citing many honors, and in 1982 the University of Kansas Press published a new edition of *Story Hour* which included several hitherto unpublished poems. A tribute written by her to Pittsburgh's Three Rivers Festival was reprinted in the 1982 *Celebration of Carnegie*.

When her brother-in-law, Kenneth Godfrey, died in 1984, the poet sent her sister these verses, read at his memorial service. (One wonders if the lines were formed at the time of Nikolai's death. . .)

"to love and cherish, till Death us do part..."
Marriage Ceremony

> Why do we date this love
> "Till Death us do part"?
> There is no sundering
> Heart and pledged heart.

Once a heart utter known,
Utterly given,
Think, could it walk alone
On earth, in heaven?

Even if flesh and bone
Fall to their sleep
Surely what Love has known
Memory can keep.

Safe, till the dark be past,
Till, on some shore,
Those we have briefly lost
Meet us once more.

Why must we date this bond
"till Death us do part"?
They are not loosed beyond
Heart and pledged heart.

Finding the responsiblity of maintaining her house and garden increasingly difficult, with her 80th birthday approaching, she put the property on the market and quickly sold it. She was spared the exhausting and sad experience of having to vacate her home of 36 years by her quiet death in her sleep July 7, 1987. In accordance with her wishes the burial service was simple and brief, with two of her poems read. But one mourner at the cemetary noticed the beauty of the butterfly hovering among the flowers and remarked that "Sally would have liked that," which so fit the lines of "Little Prayer," read by the minister of the Church of the Redemeer. Sally wrote this poem years earlier in memory of her mother.

30

Little Prayer

Because she loved the colored skies,
The gold, the bronze, the scarlet leaf,
And all bright flowers and vivid wings,
Lord, when she wakes in Paradise,
As wake she will, past age and grief,
Give her again those gay-clad things
That pleased her here; and let her choose
For raiment there no robe of white,
But one made of all rainbow hues-
Such as You lent for her delight
Before the coming of the night.

Her obituary in the Pittsburgh *Post-Gazette* recalled her illustrious career and referred to a 1959 interview: "Describing her method of writing, she said she would mull over an idea, 'usually getting the last line first.' She would craft the poem and put it aside for a few days.' Then I come back and pounce on it to see it freshly before revisions and final typing.'"

Letters to the editor from friends and admirers such as Helen Moore, creator of the program "Voices From Afar" on WQED, Pittsburgh's public television station, noted her charming wit, quoting the limerick about Lizst and The Countess. John D. Paulus, former book editor of the Pittsburgh Press, concluded: "Sara Henderson Hay's poems will be among those that will live, to give future generations a glimpse of life in America in the 20th century."

The poet wrote her own farewell more than 50 years before death silenced her voice. It appeared as the first poem in her first book and again in her

31

last book, providing the title *A Footing on This Earth.*

Dedication For a Book

I shall not lose a footing on this earth
So long as any song of mine remain:
Essential substance of my heart and brain
The valuation of my honest worth!
More of my Self will move in word and line
Than ever walked abroad in flesh and bone,
Whoever reads may be a friend of mine!
He shall perceive that I was gay, and candid,
And not too-trustful in my heart's behalf
That I was obstinate, and open-handed,
And held no grudges, and was quick to laugh;
That, clinging stubbornly to hope and breath,
I had no enmity at all for Death!

I Desire To Reason With God

EDEN

I

And the Lord God planted a garden eastward in Eden . . .
Genesis 2:8.

Behold the treacherous garden, long ago,
With the first April candidly abroad,
When docile leopard fed with trustful doe
And Eve talked nightly with a friendly God.
Behold the happy beasts—and one who was
More subtle than the rest; the spotted guise
Of Death coiled lightly in the innocent grass
Watching the woman with his lidless eyes.

Consider Eden, in those first gold days,
Sunny and green and loud with bird and bee,
How God walked softly down the murmurous
               ways—
And the Snake throve, and the disastrous Tree
Put forth its ominous freight of leaf and bud
That Eve's dark son might shed his brother's
               blood.

II

Now the serpent was more subtil than any beast of the field which the Lord God had made . . . Genesis 3: 1

"Ye shall become as Gods," the Serpent said.
And God was zealous in His own behalf.
Wherefore He smote the heavens with His
          staff
And the stars splintered, and the planets fled
And Eden trembled, and the leopards ran
Snarling into the alleys of the grass,
And mountains split to let the Lord God pass
Seeking the terrified transgressor, man.

Pity the two who cowered cheek to cheek,
Pity the disobedient pair who lay
Frightened and sick with shame and cold as
          clay.
How could they answer God? How could
          they speak?
Pity whatever poor defence they made,
Cheated by Satan, and to God betrayed.

III

And when the woman saw that the tree was good for food,
and that it was pleasant to the eyes, and a tree to be
desired to make one wise, she took of the fruit thereof . . .
Genesis 3: 6

Eve speaks:
Herein the crafty Serpent tempted me:
He said, "Ye shall be wise as God is wise;
Subtler than God intended man to be."
Wherefore I ate, and bartered Paradise.
Not for *myself*, mind you, but for my lord
Adam, who also looked upon the Tree,
I braved the angel, and despised the sword
And was desirous of a God's degree.

And here lies all the measure of my blame:
That one for whom I dreamed so proud a span
Fell short the very stature of a man,
And would not even own our common shame;
But mumbled, cringing at Jehovah's feet,
"The woman tempted me, and I did eat."

37

IV

*And the man said, "The woman whom thou gavest to be
with me, she gave me of the tree . . ."*

Genesis 3: 12

Adam speaks:
Surely, I thought, that God who stooped to dust
And fashioned me of earth, and of my flesh
Wrought the disturbing miracle afresh,
Surely that God is generous, as just.
Seeing He set the Serpent in her path
(She who was flower, and flint, and fragile air,
Gentle and wilful and withal most fair),
Might He not, so perceiving, stay His wrath?

Therefore I laid to Eve the first offence,
Hoping, as well, Jehovah might recall
How He had made her lovelier than all
Wisdom or caution or obedience.
Which futile and most desperate device
She labeled villainy and cowardice!

And the woman conceived, and bare Cain . . .
Genesis 4: 1

Consider now old Eden's tainted shoot,
That firstborn son, the child who must have
    been
Sprung from the festered bitterness between
The woman and the man; the evil fruit
Became the dark inheritance of Cain,
Poor warped, rejected, sullen demi-brute
With all the venom of that old dispute
Gall in his throat, and poison in his brain.

Conceived in anguish, and in terror born,
Drinking resentment from a flowing breast,
What fault of his, whose graceless flesh pos-
    sessed
His father's fury, and his mother's scorn?
So shaped in enmity before his birth,
Small wonder that he struck his kin to earth!

AS IT WAS IN THE BEGINNING . . .

The Brotherhood of Man, I know.
There were two brothers, long ago;
And there was precedent begun:
The stronger slew the weaker one.

39

ON CONTEMPLATING AN HONEST, ROSY-CHEEKED APPLE

Why it should suit
God's pleasure, at Creation,
To make this decent fruit
The symbol of Temptation,

Has always seemed to me
A curious deflection
From the more general harmony
Of His selection!

In Eden, were there not
Glamorous fruits growing?
Pomegranate, tangerine, apricot,
Grapes, darkly glowing?

After all's said and done,
For purpose so destructive,
Could He have chosen one
Less wantonly seductive!

THE BARGAIN

The wily serpent said to Eve
"Taste of the apple. On that day
You shall, with open eyes, percieve
Evil from good, as angels may,
As God upon His separate star."
But man has come a weary way
From Eden's flowery fields, how far,
And what he should he does not know—
For still he gropes, and argues still
In varying terms of good and ill,
Builds cities up, then lays them low,
Dreams shining dreams, betrays that trust

And grinds his brother in the dust,
Is wise and foolish, weak and strong,
Practices love and hate and lust,
Ah, what he should he does not know,
Suspended still twixt right and wrong,
Ignorant still what course to take,
Despite his bargain with the snake.

WOMAN AND SNAKE

For old acquaintance' sake
Which we in Eden made,
You need not fear, good snake,
My heel upon your head.

Of all who breathed that air
You most suited my mind;
I liked you that you were
Not humble, not kind;

But a plotter and a rebel
With a tongue smoother
For being double–
And we talked together!

Still with my blood I hear,
Oh clearer and stronger
And than all sounds lovelier,
The whisper of danger.

Is it not still our nature
To trouble, at length, God's peace?
Oh perilous, subtile creature,
I remember your voice!

NOAH

Noah, the righteous man of God,
Hurried his household to the ark
And watched the trees begin to bow
And watched the lowering sky grow dark.

He saw the driving ranks of rain
Batter the fields where he had toiled;
He saw his springing wheat go down,
His tender vineyards stripped and spoiled.

He heard the last of lightening crack
Above the world; he heard the thunder
Loud in the mountains, and he saw
The valleys and the plains go under.

He saw the fertile hillside heave
And crumble with a roaring sound,
And where his blossoming orchard stood
A steaming fissure in the ground.

He saw the pasture turn a lake,
He saw the hollows fill
And inch by inch the creeping tide
Rise from the valley to the hill.

He saw his barns begin to lean.
He heard above the shrieking wind,
The bawling of his frantic beasts
Tied in their stalls and left behind.

And he could look no more, but still
He looked, and saw the swirling brown
Relentless water reach his house,
And the wall buckle, and go down.

And Noah raised his knotted fists
And shook them at the streaming sky,
Then ground them hard against his
    mouth
To keep himself from blasphemy.

INCIDENT WITH LIONS

Into the Ark, by docile two and seven,
The obedient animals filed.
But there were some, I think, too proud,
      too wild,
Thus to be herded and driven.
Lions, surely, who shook the night with
    thunder
There on the last hill,
Drenched and bedraggled and doome
    but imperial still,
Watching the world go under.
Noah had trouble finding some of that kin
Whom he could hustle aboard.
At bay, the princely lions paced and roared
And would not save their skin.
They stood while the heavens split and the
    Flood rolled
And chose to drown deep
To the company of jackal and rat and the
    witless sheep
In the Ark's stinking hold.

THE NIGHTMARE

*. . . and Abraham . . . bound Isaac his son, and laid him
on the altar . . . and took the knife to slay his son.*
Genesis 22: 9-10

He wakens, strangling in his tears,
Again, poor child, I hear him scream
And cannot go to calm his fears.
I am the reason for the dream.

Mine is the nightmare step, the voice,
And mine the nightmare hands that
      swim
Out of the blackness toward his face—
I am the one who corners him.

He brought me flowers in his fists
To deck the altar I had made.
Even when I bound his childish wrists
He thought it was a game we played!

Oh never in his little life
Had he met fear in any guise—
He looked upon a naked knife;
He read my purpose in my eyes.

Weeping, he wakes. His mother goes
To comfort him. I make no sign.
He trembles if I come too close,
He will not trust his hand to mine.

DEFENSE

. . . if thou dost not well, sin lieth at the door.
                                        Genesis 4: 7

In whatever guise you wear,
Trouble me no more.
Naked flesh, or scale, or hair,
Quit my door!

Do you speak, or hiss, or whine,
Double tongue or one,
You shall force no will of mine–
Get you gone!

Though he stand, or coil, or crouch,
Surely Satan sees
I am safe beside my couch,
On my knees.

AS DAVID

I read it in the Holy Book–
Just such a smooth and polished stone
Young David gathered from the brook;
And with a shepherd's sling alone,
The Man of Gath was overthrown!

Now, in the current of my mind
I plunge an eager hand, and pray
That by some magic I may find
The certain stone to suit my need,
An apt and neatly rounded Creed,
A deadly, smooth Philosophy,
Wherewith to arm myself, and slay
The Philistine confronting me!

THE VICTOR

Saul hath slain his thousands,
but David his ten thousand . . .
1 Samuel 18: 7

King David's was a goodly reign,
In pious wrath he carved
Ten times a thousand breasts in twain--
Ten thousand children starved.

King David, at his God's behest,
To holy carnage rode,
And flowering red from east to west
The burning cities glowed.

This hero after God's own heart
In righteousness was mailed,
He wrenched ten thousand ribs apart,
Ten thousand women wailed.

Philistia was loud with moan
And famine stalked the land
Because so many an honest bone
Lay whitening on the sand.

But Israel sang his praise abroad
And hailed him home again,
David, the chosen one of God,
Who slew ten thousand men.

THE FAVORED

A Thousand shall fall at thy side and ten thousand at thy right hand; but it shall not come nigh thee.

Psalm 91: 7

O bless His Holy Name, indeed.
Thank Him, though half a world may bleed,
Your loves still live, your walls still stand,
He holds you in His hollowed hand.

O bless His Holy Name, rejoice.
His singled out your little voice
And heard and heeded when you cried,
Although a thousand others died.

Come, thank him on your bended knees
That you were numbered not with these
Who called on Him with equal trust
And got for answer blood and dust.

Ten thousand at your right hand fell--
But you are safe, and warm, and well
According to His loving plan
O pray and praise Him, if you can!

THE CRY

Unto the Lord this poor man cried . . .
Psalm 34: 6

"If there is any justice . . ." he kept saying,
Twisting his hands and knotting them together,
And he was only one of all the many
(Legions past numbering, time out of mind)
Who have seen all their hopes in ruin lying
And, imminent again across the blind
Indifferent sky, the driven storm clouds flying
Before the front of violent black weather.
"If there is any justice . . . " he kept praying,
As if he really thought there might be any!

BEHOLD THIS DREAMER

*. . . and Joseph dreamed another dream, and he told
it to his brethren. And they hated him yet the more . . .*

I tell you, they liked me not, from the very
      beginning.
They were banded together against me,
      eleven to one,
Although I was harmless enough, and a
      younger son,
And only given to dreams, and the reckless
      spinning
Of arrogant visions whose telling had little
      savor
For those I prophesied would bow down
      before me,
And gave me a princely robe, and his old-man's
      favor.

I was overly proud of my colorful coat, it seems,
And lacked the natural tact, or the wit, to hide it,
For my brothers' raiment was shabby and dull,
      beside it;
Moreover, I prated too often of one of my
      dreams,
And my envious brethren, liking the tale no
      whit,
Sold me a slave to Egypt because of it.

52

DELILAH

They bound, and took him south,
A year ago–and yet
I cannot quite forget
His kiss upon my mouth–
Nor his dark head that lay
Night long upon my breast–
Samson, I had not guessed
All that I could betray!

Oh he was straight of limb,
Goodly to look upon–
Humbled, in Gaza's town
What have they done to him. . . !

By day he walks in might
The chambers of my mind–
Shackled, and maimed, and blind
He comes to me by night!

FOR LOT'S WIFE

Maybe there were curtains blowing at the casement,
Maybe in the garden little leaves and new;
Jars and jars of spice in a moss-cool basement,
Maybe in the door sill a bright flower blew!

Lintel and theshold and a hearth fire burning,
God that for this tending fashioned womankind,
If You bade her leave them, and never be returning
How could You expect her not to look behind!

THE WOUND

*And one shall say unto him, What are these wounds
in thine hands? Then he shall answer, Those with
which I was wounded in the house of my friends.*
Zechariah 13: 6

I will wash this wound, and bind it with honey
      and oil.
I will say "It is nothing. Let it be. The bleeding
      will stop."
Knowing I lie in my teeth, that it will not heal
Nor soon, nor ever. It has been torn too deep.
The dark stains widen . . . I think there is no
      balm
That the cool mind can bring, no skill, no art
To close this ragged horror in my palm,
To quench the bright blood pounding from
      the heart.

THE SURVIVOR

When I went through the wilderness
Sustenance, of a sort, I found,
Meager and scanty though it was
Upon that graceless ground.

It did not hang like fruit on trees,
There were no trees in that scarred land;
I sought it on my hands and knees
Among the rocks and sand.

It was no proper kind of food,
That simple Wanting Not To Die,
But every little scrap was good,
So ravenous was I.

And if my pillow was a shard,
From stripped sheer weariness I slept,
And grown so muscular and hard,
How light, how fierce I stepped!

Another Exodus like that
I could not make, and live. And yet
In a green land, and warm, and fat,
I think and think on it . . . .

THE DAILY MANNA

There is nothing at all besides this manna . . . !
Complaint of the children of Israel,   Numbers 11: 6

If suddenly, wonderfully, glittering among
           the leaves,
The fabled, the gilded phoenix would break
           from cover!
But here is only a small, brown-breasted bird
           that grieves
In a few plaintive notes at dusk, over and
           over . . . .

Oh, if a milk-white unicorn would appear
And stamp with silver hooves at the edge of
           the meadow!
But that which moves near the birches is only
           deer
Dappled with light and shadow.

I wish I could take three steps into an enchanted
           wood!
But this is only the grove where the lovers come
At evening, the whispering boys and girls; only
           the valley road,
The short way home . . . .

THE SHAPE GOD WEARS

... But ask now the beasts, and they shall teach thee;
and the fowls of the air, and they shall tell thee . . . .

So questing, I was bold to dare
The sinewy tiger in his lair.
"Come forth, striped Sir, make known to me
What God it was who fashioned thee?"

Outleapt he like a muscled blaze,
Patterned in black and gold he was.
"Jehovah is His name," he cried,
"Tiger of Tigers, beryl-eyed.

Flat flanked and sleek, His paws are curled
About the margins of the world.
He stalketh in His jungles grim.
I, even I, am like to Him."

I sought that moving mountainside,
The elephant, with ears fanned wide,
Treading the forests. "Sir, tell me
What manner of a God made thee?"

He swirled his trunk about an oak
And wrenched it up before he spoke,
Then answered in a trumpet blast
"Old Super-Pachyderm, that vast

Lord of the Elephants–the great
Trampler upon the worm's estate.
Crag-shouldered, terrible is He
Who of his substance fashioned me."

I scaled the precipice, to seek
The eagle on his drafty peak.
"Tell me, O Gazer at the sun,
The nature of that mighty one

"Your Lord." He turned his crested head
And screamed athwart the wind, and said
"Ancient of Eagles, wild and free,
Rider of Tempests, He made me.

His wing is stretched above the thunder,
His claws can rip the hills asunder.
His beak of two hooked knives is made.
Look on His likeness–be afraid!"

Then turned I to the whorléd snail
Whose house is exquisite and frail,
Most deftly wrought, "Sir, I would know
What God it was who shaped thee so."

Then cried he proudly to my face
"Eternal Snail, God of my race.
The lightening in His silvery track,
He wears the world upon His back.

He is most beautiful and wise,
He dwelleth in the moisty skies,
In the grey wall at heaven's rim,
And He has made me after Him."

Then laughed I in superior mirth.
"Attend, ye creatures of the earth,
Misled, mistaken, all undone
And self-deceivers, ever one.

Hear ye, deluded beasts while I
Explain the shape God wears, and why.
Self-evident the truth's displayed.
He is *my* father, sirs," I said,
"And in my image He is made!"

THESE HANDS

In the image of God created he him . .
Genesis 1: 27

These hands are shaped like God's, and so
Let them be careful what they do.

Let them be quick to lift the weak,
Let them be kind as they are strong,
Let them defend the silent meek
Against the many-languaged wrong.

These hands are shaped like God's. Be sure
They bear the mark of no man's pain
Who asked their help to make secure
His little roof–and asked in vain.

These hands are shaped like God's. Take care
They catch the sparrow hurled from air.

Lest God look down from Heaven, and see
What things are wrought beneath the sun
By us, His images, and be
Ashamed of what His hands have done.

MAN'S BEHALF

. . . suffer me a little, and I will shew thee that
I have yet to speak on (man's) behalf . . . Job 36: 2

Despite man's grievous ravaging of man,
For all the bloody mark upon his brow,
Give him his due. Remembering he began
A weaker beast than most, regard him now.
Is it not past believing that he stands
Straddling the world? Is it not past belief
That he should take the lightening in his hands,
That he should hold the sea itself in fief?

He *can* draw out Leviathan with an hook.
He sets his flimsy heel upon the cloud.
For all his violence, his perversity,
Hail what he is, and hail what he shall be.
Pity his crimes against himself, but look
On this incredible creature, and be proud.

JACOB SINGS

Better than valleys, and the narrow grace
Of willows leaning to the river's face,
The terrible, male beauty of this place.

Better than vineyards is the brawny sand,
And the stout breathing of this lusty land,
Wind in the ears, and the sky on either
       hand!

I have abjured the subtle-bosomed south,
And the soft rains, like honey on the mouth,
Here is a muscled fasting, and a drouth.

For I have found the grape too sickly sweet,
And I am wearied of the docile wheat–
But here, if one be strong enough, is meat!

And brave life, Israel, for the spirit grown
Wakeful and fierce . . . and many a man has
       known
A harder pillow than an honest stone.

THE BEASTS

And the beasts of the field be at peace with thee . . .

Job 5: 23

Oh think—the satin-skinned, the dappled,
The doe with her fawn
Standing at gaze, calm-eyed, untroubled,
Their terror gone.

Think—the round rabbit, the plumed
     squirrel,
The lynx, too,
And the wolf, forgetful of his quarrel
With man, with you.

Even the curved panther, he
With knives along his jaw—
How soft that heavy chin upon your knee,
And his furled paw!

IN THE LION'S DEN

Dear Daniel, do not be afraid.
Between these scowling beasts and you
Is set a heavenly barricade,

A wall invisible, but strong;
They cannot scale it, nor break through,
Though they essay it, all night long.

It is disquieting, I know,
This constant padding to and fro,
But try to put it out of mind;
The wall is very well designed.
Poor Daniel, do not tremble so!
It really doesn't mean a thing,
The way they crouch, as if to spring–
Good Heavens! Down, sir! Let it go!

ELEGY

There is an evil among all things that are done under the sun, that there is one event unto all . . . Ecclesiastes 9: 3

Take gently in your hand, Enormous Death,
This fledgling sparrow fallen from the nest,
And gather to your breast
A bird that never flew, nor ever sung,
It was so small, so young.
Was there no creature weary of it breath
Lying broken in your path
For you to lean above
And minister to, in pity and in love,
That you, in your huge harvest, could not pass
A trembling sparrow, huddled in the grass?

Indifferent Death, I do indeed forget
Your empty eyes that make no reasoned choice,
Your ears that heed no voice.
As well implore the unpersuadable wind
As ask Death to be kind,
Or plead with rain, or the blind waves entreat,
As Death, who never yet
Has any bargain made
Nor been from his unpurposed purpose swayed;
To whose impartial hands, since Time began,
As one are fallen sparrow and fallen man.

SWEET STORY OF OLD

JOSEPH TO MARY

Mary, Beloved, if I wounded you
With clumsy silence, or with tardy speech,
It was because my heart was slow to reach
Beyond the limits of its mortal view!
Not that I doubted you, or loved you less—
But it was hard to face the winking town,
And a man's pride is difficult to down,
Whatever faith he may, in truth, profess!

How many nights I watched you, as you lay
With this the Holy Child upon your breast;
What tumult shook my heart from day to day!
Oh little Mary, have you never guessed
That I, who would have died to spare you harm,
So feared to clasp you with an earthly arm?

MARY TO JOSEPH

This dread has been upon me, chilled and numbing
This fear has sat within me, from the start,
Since first I told you of the angel's coming,
And of the Child that lay beneath my heart!

It was no easy thing to understand,
And not by word or deed have you reproved me—
But Joseph, Joseph—when you took my hand,
Did you believe me, even as you loved me?

THE GIFTS

So Mary put the gifts away,
But the strange words she kept–
And wakeful many a night she lay
While goodman Joseph slept.

"Frankincense for a king . . ." she thought
"A crown for a king's head–
Was ever such rich treasure brought
Down to a manger bed?"

But once she clasped the Child to her
And kissed His narrow feet,
Remembering the subtle myrrh
That scents a winding sheet.

CHRISTMAS, THE YEAR ONE A.D.

That year no wondering shepherds came,
Nor ever any more
The Magi from the glamorous East
Crowding the narrow door.

There were not gifts of myrrh or gold,
Or jewels in glittering strands
Too heavy for a child to hold,
Too harsh for baby hands.

But Martha baked a barley cake,
Dorcas a spicy bun,
And goodman Joseph carved a toy
For Mary's little Son.

Timothy brought a woolly lamb,
Esther a fluted shell,
And all day long came friendly folk
To wish young Jesus well.

There was no sudden clash of steel
To make sweet Mary start,
Nor any dark, ambiguous words
Coiling about her heart.

Only the things of home, and peace,
With the calm stars above.
And little Jesus safe among
The holier gifts of love.

MARY

That day the small Christ hurt his hand
Upon a rusty nail,
Joseph could never understand
Why Mary grew so pale

And why she sat, with drooping head
And eyes gone dark with pain,
Long after he was comforted
And sent to play again—

Or why, long after day was done,
And all the household slept,
She knelt beside her little Son
And clasped her hands, and wept.

IN NAZARETH

And he went down with them, and came to
Nazareth, and was subject unto them. But his mother
kept all these sayings in her heart . . .   Luke 2: 51

Our son, who spoke so bravely in the temple
To the wise doctors and the learned men
Came home with us. In Nazareth again
He and my Joseph went about the simple
Business of carpentry, and he grew stronger
And taller day by day, and the years flew--
Such busy, happy years, and ah so few
Till suddenly he was a child no longer.

And I remembered every curious saying,
Watching him, knowing he was set apart
Even from the time he lay beneath my heart.
Sometimes I thought I saw a strange light play
About his head, and felt my heart grow cold
Seeing him heave an oak beam to his shoulder.

WHERE ARE THE NINE?

There were ten men of Galilee
Christ healed of an infirmity.
There were ten men He paused to bless,
And one came back, in thankfulness.
There was but one, who knelt and heard
His kind, tired word:
"Were not ten healed? Ten that were Mine?
Where are the nine . . .?"

"Lord who art walking still with
Christ Who hast healed men ten times ten.
Thou Who hast cleansed and made me free,
Have I so soon forgotten Thee?
Thou Who hast made my leprous soul
Every whit whole,
Help me to say, "Lord, here is Thine,
One of the nine . . ."

THE PRODIGAL

They made a feast in the banquet hall,
And the calf was slain for the prodigal.
And here I sit, while the last guests linger,
With a robe on my back, and a ring on my
      finger.

Well, home calls somehow, the whole world
      through,
And its threshold portal is a dream come true,
And the glow of the home hearth is beautiful to
      see
When one has been a vagrant, in a Far Country.

Oh it's not much fun to be swine herd keeping,
And to bed with the hard earth is cold enough
      sleeping,
And after the husks were gone, I fasted–
But Oh my friends–while the money lasted!

THE PRODIGAL

Was it worth so much to me, then, to be warmed,
    to be fed?
I do not remember how it feels to be cold,
Nor to hunger for more than this meat and these
    dates and this bread
By my father doled.

I was headstrong and wilful and foolish, they all
    knew it,
But have I forgotten how kindly I was met?
Not for a moment; indeed, my brother sees to it
That I do not forget.

I am clipped and fat and tame as a barnyard fowl,
Was it this that I wanted, there in the swineherd's
    shack?
Well, I made my choice–but I know in my heart, in
    my soul,
I should never have come back!

THE ELDER SON

I say unto you, that likewise joy shall be in heaven over one sinner that repenteth, more than over ninety and nine just persons, which need no repentence.   Luke 15: 7

What profit hath the Elder Son,
Toiling amid his father's walls,
If, since the world was first begun,
Feasts have been laid for prodigals

Who put away their threadbare sin
And stagger home, repentance voicing?
Even the angels hail them in
With what a ratio of rejoicing!

WITNESS FOR THE DEFENCE

I am the Elder Brother; and that one
Who, having borne all day the heat of the sun,
Begrudged the equal penny given a neighbor
For his eleventh-hour labor.

Among that provident company am I
Whose lamps were burning high,
Who clustered in about the Wedding Table
With time and oil to spare. And in the fable
I am that thrifty spinster, the Rich Ant,
Who told the mendicant
Grasshopper to go and dance the winter through.
And I am Martha, too,
Bustling about the kitchen and dairy,
Complaining to my Friend, nagging at Mary.

Self-righteous, petty, stingy and unkind,
All these am I, grasping and mean of mind,
And these unlovely attributes serve well
As posts whereon to pin the parable,
While I see to it that the fields are tilled,
The harvest gathered in, the granary filled,
The vineyard planted and the hearthstone swept,
The tithes and taxes paid, the farmstead kept.

THE FATHER

Well, he's come home, this younger son of mine,
But something in his penitence betrays
He had been guardian of fouler swine,
Before those latter days . . . .

For there's a furtive something sliding under
His speech; he sits and twists his ring around
And stares at it. My son was lost--I wonder,
Is he so truly found?

Oh I am glad I did not hesitate
To run and clasp him hard in my embrace.
Still, it was rather more than fortunate
He could not see *my* face.

THE CHILD

*And Jesus called a little child unto him and set
him in the midst of them . . .*   Matthew 18: 2

Though it was long ago
And I so young and small
As it were yesterday
So clear can I recall

His face, his speaking eyes,
And how he stooped to me
And took me in his arms
And set me on his knee.

I knew, as children know,
That he was kind and good,
And that he was my friend,
Although I understood

Not half of what he said
About his father's home,
Where those of childlike heart
And childlike faith should come.

But I remember well
His gentle voice, the way
He smiled—and how I wept
When I was led away!

CANA OF GALILEE

As fine a jam as ever man was in.
My daughter's wedding—only child, you know
The apple of our eye—As I was saying,
The wine ran low.

Well, you can just imagine how I felt,
With not a dealer open in the town
And the wife throwing forty fits and swearing
We'd never live it down.

All the important Pharisees were there,
All of the Scribes and rulers, more or less,
And what the local gossip would have been,
It isn't hard to guess.

I don't expect you to believe the story,
But here it is: in fine,
The steward came and said six jars of water
Were turned to wine.

You could have knocked me over with a feather,
But when I caught my breath
I asked who did it, and he said, some stranger,
He thought from Nazareth;

But why or how he'd done the favor for me
The steward couldn't tell.
I've often wondered who the fellow was—
By God, I'd pay him well!

JAIRUS' DAUGHTER

*And he cometh to the house of the ruler, and seeth the tu-
mult, and them that wept and wailed greatly . . . and he saith
unto them, why make ye this ado, and weep? The damsel is not
dead, but sleepeth. And they laughed him to scorn.*

*But when he had put them all out, he taketh the father and
the mother of the damsel, and entereth in where she was lying.
And he took the damsel by the hand and said unto her . . . Damsel, I say unto thee, arise. And straightway she arose . .*

Mark 5: 38-41

There was a cloth about my head,
There was a bandage on my eyes;
Through my closed ears I heard his voice. He
        said
"She sleeps . . ." He said "Arise."

Deep in my dream I heard, and so
Listening, obeyed. He took my hand.
I think he has the kindest face I know . . .
I think he is my friend.

They ask such silly things, those men
With beards, and all the village folk.
I tell them patiently, over and over again,
"He called me, and I woke . . ."

I wish he would come back our way
I watch the road when it grows light,
And when I blow my candle out I say,
"Sleep well . . ." to him . . . "Goodnight . . . ."

82

REMINISCENCE

*Jesus said unto him, "Sell all thou hast, and
distribute it to the poor, and come, follow me."
And when he heard this he was very sorrowful,
for he was very rich.*   Luke 18: 22,23

Yes, I remember, long ago,
A wandering teacher came our way.
Some said he was a man of God
And word of him was spread abroad,
So I went down from Galilee
Mostly from curiosity
To hear what he might say.

He had a strange persuasive charm
Which went completely to my head;
For I inclined to youth's extremes,
Fine altruistic hopes and dreams,
I even reached the point where I
Wanted to join his company
And follow where he led.

Thank God I thought it over twice!
A most impractical whim–
For I have had a goodly life,
I have six sons, a virtuous wife,
Yea, I am rich in flocks and land,
And these are jewels on my hands,
I wonder what became of him . . . .

INCIDENT IN GETHSEMANE

I am the snake in Eden cursed
For that old mischief with the Tree.
And in this grove, Gethsemane,
A quiet garden, like the first,
I coiled myself upon a stone,
Waiting to see what I should see.
I saw a young man, all alone,
Who knelt and cried upon God's name,
Stifling his moan, as a man must.
And out of pity for Your son
(Though of *Your* pity I had none)
Creeping upon my belly I came
And with my flickering tongue I kissed
His naked heel, and harmless, laid
On his worn sandal, in the dust,
My unregenerate, dangerous head.

Remember it, Mine Enemy!

IN THE SERVANTS' HALL

. . . And Peter followed afar off. And when they had kindled a fire in the midst of the hall, and were set down together, Peter sat down among them. But a certain maid beheld him as he sat by the fire, and earnestly looked upon him, and said, This man was also with him. And he denied him, saying, Woman I know him not.   Luke 22:54-57

When first he answered me, I knew he lied.
The cloak about his shame was much too thin
To hide it from a woman's eyes. Beside,
I saw him, when they brought the prisoner in

Following afar off. And yet to seek
Another proof, I looked at him and said
"This man was also with him. Let him speak
And he betrays himself." He shook his head

And turned away. By nature being perverse
For very spite I asked again. Alack,
The fellow turned on me with such a curse
That even I, a kitchen wench, fell back.

They left at cock-crow. *That* for such as he!
But of the man whom he denied as friend,
One thing I know--had he so looked at me,
I would have followed him, to the world's
       end . . .

BALLAD OF SIMON THE CYRENIAN

And when they had mocked him, they took off the purple from him, and put his own clothes on him, and led him out to crucify him.

And they compel one Simon, a Cyrenian, who passed by coming out of the country, the father of Alexander and Rufus, to bear his cross for him.　　　　　Mark 15: 20,21

Dragging feet and weary eyes,
　　Pity, pity them—
Hot and white the highway lies
　　From Jerusalem!

Merchant out of Galilee
　　Come from far away.
Simon the Cyrenian
　　Going home to-day.

They that take a homeward path
　　Do not tarry when
Father's arms so long to clasp
　　Little sons again!

Thus he counts the weary miles
　　While the highway crawls
Like a creeping dusty snake
　　to the City walls.

On and on, and nearer home
　　Hold a moment—wait—
Who are these the rabble leads
　　From the City gate?

86

Pitiless the blinding road,
    Pitiless the sky–
Only Roman prisoners
    Going forth to die?

Staggering with shame and pain
    Streaked with dust and sun,
Two who bear the brand of thief
    And another One.

Make a place amid the crowd,
    Look on him again–
Simon, see, his shoulder bleeds
    Where the cross has lain!

And the scourge has seamed his back
    Bruised and raw and red–
Strange, that he should wear a brier
    Plaited round his head–

Simon, look–he stumbled there,
    For his eyes are dim;
Be a man, and help a Man
    Bear his cross for him!

Shadows of the afternoon
    Fall across the way–
Simon the Cyrenian
    Going home to-day.

Longer in the traveling
  Than he thought to be,
Since his feet retraced the road
  Up to Calvary.

Simon, did you dream, that night,
  Of a journey done;
That another Father clasped
  A beloved Son?

Did you know how blest you were?
  Would that he had been
Merchant out of Galilee,
  Simon of Cyrene!

NIGHT OF CALVARY

. . . and the earth did quake, and the rocks rent;
and the graves were opened. . .   Matthew 27: 51-52

Suddenly, on the shaken earth
Thick darkness dropped like lead,
And startled sepulchers cast forth
The rude-awakened dead.

Shuddering from the graves they came,
Stumbling on fleshless fleet,
Each clasping to his shrunken frame
His moldy winding sheet.

They clicked across the shivering plain,
They crowded here and there,
Frightened to find themselves again
In the forgotten air.

Across the blackened world they fled
Through mire and field and fell,
The pitiful, bewildered dead,
Looking for Gabriel.

And when the livid light returned
Each where his grave had been
Stood whimpering in the chill, and yearned
To lay him down therein.

Each, fumbling, stretched his narrow girth
On the unfeeling stones,
Till by and by the kindly earth
Sheltered the timid bones,

Covered them from the impious day
And closed each hollow eye.
But taut and terrified they lay
Palpitant still they lie,

They quiver at the roar of rain,
Wakeful in dust they cower—
How could they ever sleep again,
Remembering that Hour?

THE SILENT

. . . the common people heard him gladly
Mark 12:37

That day the dreadful story ran
On lightning feet through lane and mart,
White wrath rose hot in many a man
Who dared not speak his heart.

What grievous fury sat concealed
In many an honest beggar's eyes;
How many a cripple Christ had healed
Stared dumbly at the skies.

How many a leper, cleansed and whole
Stood tight-lipped in that murderous crowd
And knew the anguish of a soul
That dares not cry aloud.

How many a simple fellow saw
The brutal travesty of right,
And cursed the Council, and the Law,
Behind his door, that night.

How many a woman bowed her head,
How many a mother, long awake,
Lay wide-eyed on a sleepless bed
For gentle Mary's sake.

THE UPPER ROOM

. . . then came Jesus, the doors being shut, and stood in the midst, and said " Peace be unto you . . ."   John 20: 26

In the heart's house, my cautious soul and I
Assured ourselves of many a bolt and bar,
We left no latch for any hand to try,
No careless casement wide, no door ajar.
The curtains hid us from the monstrous sky
From the enormous presence of the gloom,
But we were fearful, though we knew not why,
Facing each other in that quiet room.

And so we dragged stout Logic to the door
And braced it fast, and tied the shutters hard
With tough-thonged Reason for our Faith,
        worn thin,
And turned, hearing a footfall on the floor,
For, with each entrance doubly locked and
        barred,
Suddenly came the Christ, and stood therein.

ENTRANCE INTO HEAVEN

And truly the Son of Man goeth, as it was determined--
Luke 22 :22

Down the white steps of Heaven Christ came to
     meet him,
That soul with rope-galled throat and stricken
     eyes,
Hastened with glad and outstretched hands to
     greet him,
And led him proudly into Paradise!

Christ said "Thou, too, hast known
     Gethsemane,
Condemned for what the world accounted not
Obedience! That shame *required* of thee
Wilt thou forgive, my friend Iscariot?"

AFTER THE CRUCIFIXION

Except ye become as little children . . . .

We were the children Jesus loved.
Jonathan sat upon His knee
That morning in the marketplace
Of Galilee.

Benjamin was the little boy
Who had the lunch of fish and bread
Which Jesus blessed–and Benjamin saw
Five thousand fed.

And Miriam was sick, and slept
And would not wake–and she can tell
How Jesus came and took her hand,
And she was well!

We were all children, everywhere,
Who looked upon His face. We knew,
That day they told us He had died,
It was not true.

We wondered why our parents wept
And doubted Him and were deceived
For we remembered what He said,
And *we* believed!

THE NEIGHBORS

And he . . . came into his own country . . . and when the sab-
bath day was come, he began to teach . . . . and many hearing
him were astonished, saying, From whence hath this man
these things? . . . Is not this the carpenter, the son of Mary, the
brother of James, and Joses, and of Juda, and Simon? and are not
his sisters here with us? And they were offended at him.
   But Jesus said unto them, A prophet is not without honor, but
in his own country, and among his own kin, and in his own
house.   Mark 6: 1-4

News of the trouble in Jerusalem,
His trial, and the manner of his death,
Came to his own village, and to his neighbors,
The people of Nazareth.

They talked. "His mother'll take it pretty hard.
She set great store by him--though I must say
He treated her, at least to *my* way of thinking,
In a mighty high-handed way."

"Why, you remember the time, he was just a boy,
He give them such a scare?
Lost himself three days in Jerusalem
And never turned a hair

When they found him, but answered back, as cool
        as you please,
He was doing his father's business, or some such
        truck,
As if most of us hadn't known his father, Joseph,
Since he was knee high to a duck.

95

And *his* business was carpentry, not talking back
    to priests!"
But Mary, she always remembered it. Some claim
She was a little bit touched–had visions and all–
Before he came."

She was always partial to him, but if you ask *me*
He'd a been a better son
If he'd stayed home and raised a family
Like his brothers done."

"The trouble with him, he didn't use his judgment.
He was forever speaking out,
Though many's the time I've told him: there's
            some wrong things
Folks just don't talk about."

They say, though, in some parts of the country
He drew quite a crowd. Five thousand or more.
        I don't know–
Here in Nazareth nobody'd walk two blocks to hear
        him,
And it probably ain't so."

"It's hard on his family, the disgrace and all.
And I'm sorry about him. I was his friend.
I liked him, you understand. But I always said
He'd come to a bad end."

BALLAD OF THE GOLDEN BOWL

"What is this golden bowl, mother,
With its strange design?
It is not like our other things,
But foreign, and fine . . . "

"It came out of the East, child,
A long time ago.
Your grandmother gave it to us.
This is all we know:

When your father's brother was born
On a winter's night,
A new star stood in the skies–
It was a great sight!

And three kings rode from afar
To kneel at his bed.
They were seeking a greater King,
Or so they said . . . "

"And was he a King, mother,
 My father's kin?"
"No, child. It was all a mistake.
It must have been . . .

For they went away, those three,
And they came no more.
And he had a sad life, child,
He died poor . . ."

"Had he a wife, mother,
And a boy of his own?"
"He had neither chick nor child, darling
He was all alone.

He was a good man,
But he came to grief,
And they hanged him on a cross
Like a common thief."

"But why, mother, why?
If he was kind and good?"
"It was a plot of some sort, child,
We never understood.

There was nothing we could do,
    Being humble folk.
He was your grandmother's favorite.
Her heart broke.

She gave us this golden bowl
When she came to die.
It is sad--it is all we have
To remember him by . . . ."

HELP THOU MY UNBELIEF

SURELY I WOULD SPEAK TO THE ALMIGHTY

Surely I would speak to the Almighty,
and I desire to reason with God . . .

. . . help Thou my unbelief . . .

Most poignant of all please, this desperate reaching
After a God, a Faith, a saving care
One is not even sure exists–beseeching
The thing unproved to prove that it is there.

Oh pitiful irony, that men so need
So want a God for gratitude or grief
They first construct, then ask that God to heed
"Lord, I believe–help Thou my unbelief."

DILEMMA

The program of Redemption is disturbing
To one who unaccountably was given
A skeptic heart incapable of curbing
Its reckless theorizing Hell and Heaven;
Their puzzling fees and standards of admission—
Who finds a certain tinge of humor blent
In Eden's most calamitous fruition,
And God's celestial predicament!

Bewildering alternatives–to grope
Along the maze of Cant and Creed and Schism,
To clutch a Faith as it had been a rope,
And I in drowning's final paroxysm
Or turn with vast naiveté to Hope,
The soul's indomitable optimism!

THE REASON

The heart has its reasons . . .
Numbers 22:23, 24

The burdened heart, beneath its load,
Sees clearest, with the eyes of faith.
Not Balaam, but the beast he rode,
Perceived the presence in the path.

O mounted Mind, thou Whip-in-Hand,
Be patient in this latter day.
If this thy creature stubborn stand,
Perchance some angel bars the way.

FOR A CERTAIN KINDLY ATHEIST

His heart's Jerusalem of doubt
I cannot ask that Thou condone—
But if he cast Thy prophets out,
He flung no stone.

He led them to the City gates,
And bade them bind their sandals on,
And gave them bread and wine and dates,
Before he said "Begone!"

SATAN SAID

And there came a day when the Sons of God gathered them-
selves together to present themselves before the Lord, and
Satan came along among them. And the Lord said unto Satan,
"Whence comest thou?"
And Satan answered the Lord, and said "From going to and fro
in the world, and from walking up and down in it!"   Job 1: 13

Up and down, up and down in the world.
To and fro–
Was it You that twirled
Your cane idly, so–
Yesterday, on the Avenue?
Was it You
Across the theatre aisle,
Bold with disguise
Of a sleek smile,
And little glinting eyes
Of a strange blue?
Was it You

Shoulder to shoulder, swirled
With the crowd? Do you go
Up and down, up and down in the world,
To and fro–
Nonchalant, unrevealed
To the Sons of God,
With your horns concealed,
And your hooves shod?

SIC TRANSIT

The Cities of the Plain are dust;
Assyria is fox's plunder;
Sidon and Tyre to silence thrust,
Nineveh fallen, with fire and thunder.
Across the margin of the world
The drift of Babylon is swirled,
And centuries of rot and rust
Have gnawed Capernaum asunder.

Stone crumbles–but more staunchly fares
A dust incredibly translated:
Judas still haggles at his wares,
Cain is forever new-created.
Delilah, in a Paris frock,
Goes out to tea at five o'clock.
Salome climbs the Subway stairs,
Potiphar takes the Elevated.

ACCUSATION

. . . what man is there of you, whom if his son
ask him for bread, will he give him a stone . . .?
Matthew 7: 9

But this man starved before he died,
(For all Your Word assures.)
Did You not hear him when he cried?
Was he no child of Yours?

Where were You, yesterday,
Between the Cherubim,
Turning Your cloudy face away,
Stretching no hand to him.

TEXT

Because I heard His ways were just
In God's strong hand I placed my trust.

I saw a child born lame and blind.
I saw a man of honest mind
In his own house despoiled and slain
By thieves who lived to spoil again.

I saw a woman's honor sold
By her own lovely hand, for gold
She flourished to her life's soft close,
While homely virtue starved and froze.

I saw the meek, accepting dearth,
Fall heir to some six feet of earth,
But arrogance did not hesitate
To claim the whole of man's estate.

Charity furrowed his dry plain
While on greed's acres fell God's rain.
Truth withered in a rocky cleft,
With bay trees blossoming right and left.

I saw how red the rivers ran
Where man struck down his brother man . . .
Ten million murders brought to pass
All by the jawbone of an ass.

I found another verse, which read
More to my credence, for it said
Briefly, with less to re-arrange
For faith's sad eyes: "His ways are strange."

DE PROFUNDIS

Lord, I have lost my way, who was so sure.
My candle gutters to a glimmering spark–
I cannot long endure
The terror, and the dark.

Father, my plumes are bowed;
My arrogant sword is shattered, hilt and blade.
I am no longer proud,
I am afraid.

Wilt Thou forgive the pride,
The foolish mockery I flung at Thee,
And let me come, as children do, and hide
My face against Thy knee?

Wilt Thou forget the passion, and the pain,
Give back the simple heart whose faith sufficed,
That questioned not? And let me find again
My brother, Christ?

THE SEARCH

I sought Him where my logic lead.
"This friend is always sure and right.
His lamp will give sufficient light.
I need no Star," I said.

I sought Him in the city square,
Logic and I went up and down
The marketplace of many a town,
But He was never there.

I tracked Him in the mind's far rim;
The clever intellect went forth
To east and west and south and north
But found no trace of Him.

We walked the world from sun to sun,
Logic and I, and Little Faith,
But never came to Nazareth,
Nor met the Holy One.

We sought in vain. And finally
Back to the heart's small house I crept
And fell upon my knees and wept.
And Lo! He came to me!

PRAYER TO MARY

Holy Mary, God's Mother,
Wilt thou look from Heaven,
Thou who wast a woman too,
Grant that I be given
Such sweet measure of thy grace,
Such white strength of thee,
As my slender soul may wear,
Well, and fittingly!
Walk with me these troubled days,
Till the dark be past,
That I need not drop my gaze,
Meeting thine, at last!

COMMUNION

With the living wine and bread
Freely, freely was I fed,
Bountifully nourished.

Wherefore I beseech thee, Lord,
Turn from Heaven thy dwelling place-
I would spread my own small board
With the measure of thy grace.

With the store that I posess
Of thy great unselfishness,

Harvest of the faithful seed
Sown against my spirit's need.

Such good portion as is mine
of thy charitable vine;

Milk of kindliness, the curd
Of the unoffending word;

Olives from the gentle tree
Rooted in humility,

Tolerant vintage of the soul,
Sturdy meat of self-control,

Fruit of patience, firm and fair,
And the goodly bread of prayer.

Father, I extend to thee
This, my hospitality.

 I have set my hearth alight,
Spread the linen smooth and white,
Wilt thou sup with me, tonight?

THE DIFFERENCE

Charity is silent, Charity is content
To have said in silence everything Love meant.
Charity does not seek
A phrase, but sets warm lips upon the cheek.
Even if it rejoice
Love needs no speech, but Rancor wants a voice
And tirelessly will rehearse
Its grievance, chapter and verse.
Love's mute, and willingly so, but do not doubt
Anger's articulate, and will speak out.
Charity holds its peace, but be assured
Bitterness knows a final, ruinous word,
And Bitterness will, at any cost, be heard.

HIC IACET

I

Epitaph for a Certain Gentleman

Here lieth one whose fleshly lust
Did always his meek spirit lead.
Now, meditating in the dust,
He finds it comforting to trust

A Christ Who was not too divine
To recognize a human need.
But went with publicans to dine,
And turned the water into wine.

THE FIRE

I like the building of an open fire
But for one feature:
Inevitably, as the flame licks higher
Wrapping the logs, there scuttles from a crack
Some minute but distinguishable creature
Smoked from his room,
Who halts, appalled, sniffs Doom,
Ducks hastily back,
Is driven forth, runs, desperate, that way and this,
Is blocked by an abyss,
Stops, wavering, in his track,
Falls, struggles, shrivels, dies,
Before my eyes.

This harrowing spectacle *I* cannot view
Unwrenched by pity. Though, if accounts be true,
A like reaction, at a Later Day
Should not be expected, Father in Heaven, of You.

THE FIGHT

O Death, how bitter is the remembrance of thee
to a man who is at peace with his possessions . . .
Apocrypha

But not to him alone
Whose happy breath is drawn
In peace amid his lands,
With plenty in his hands
The thought of Death is bad.

To him, as well, whose life
Is anguished and unsafe,
And whose possessions' scope
Is nothing but his hope,
The face of Death is still
Most to be shunned, and vile.

For even if he cry
In his extremest day
"Sweet Death . . ." He lies! He lies!
Himself that speech denies.
His every part shall strive
To keep that man alive.

His will gives no assent
To the supreme affront;
He clings with desperate strength
To living's breadth and length.
And when the will has done,
The stubborn flesh fights on.

THE HAPPY LAND

A melodious noise of birds in the spreading branches,
a running that could not be seen of skipping beasts.
All the world shined with clear light, and none was
hindered in his labor.   Apocrypha

Where is that happy land, oh where
In what country of the mind?
And may one rise and journey there
And dwell among this pleasant kind?
Say, would that wayworn wanderer find
Freedom and peace and balm for care
In such a golden light as shined
On Eden, through an earlier air?

Oh might he build a little house
With his own hands, and turn the sod,
Unhindered work, and play, and feast--
Friends with himself, and with his God,
With them that sing among the boughs,
And every soft-eyed, skipping beast?

ONE HESITANT

. . . but we shall all be changed, in a moment,
in the twinkling of an eye, at the last trump.

1 Corinthians 15: 52

But this known body, this familiar shell,
Follows the angles of my soul so well!
Having been worn thus long and comfortably,
It has become too integrally *me*.

I am afraid on that Final Day,
Stripped of its threadbare but beloved clay,
And stared at by a radiant angel band,
Self-conscious and abashed my soul will stand

Wanting again the shabby flesh it had,
So stiff and strange, in its white raiment clad!

BEGINNER

Now the page is almost turned
On the lesson I have learned.
On the most that I have known:
My familiar flesh and bone
Level eyes and lifted chin,
Every part of me that is
Written legibly within
This concise parenthesis
Birth, and Death; the two extremes
Of my mortal paragraph
Dotted with an epitaph.

Where I must now, it seems,
Turn my wits and set my hand
To a newer lexicon,
Striving hard to understand
Primary Oblivion,
In the text assigned to me,
Primer of Eternity

"THEREFORE WITH ANGELS
AND ARCHANGELS. . ."

*. . . Therefore with Angels and Archangels and with all the
company of Heaven, we laudand magnify Thy glorious name.*

Book of Common Prayer

Lord, Thou art kind, indeed,
To such as cry to Thee,
Permitting them to enter in
This goodly Company,

But Oh more gracious far,
That Thou dost not disown
The smallest, rapt-eyed, trembling soul
Speechless, before Thy throne.